BOUND BY HONOR

A MAFIOSO'S STORY

BILL BONANNO

ST. MARTIN'S PRESS ❧ NEW YORK

Endpaper photo: Bill and Joe Bonanno in 1936.

Library of Congress Cataloging-in-Publication Data

Bonanno, Bill.
    Bound by honor : a mafioso's story / Bill Bonanno.—1st ed.
        p.   cm.
    ISBN 0-312-20388-8
    1. Bonanno, Bill.   2. Mafia—New York (State)—New York—
Biography.   3. Organized crime—New York (State)—New York.
I. Title.
HV6452.N7B65   1999
364.1'092—dc21   99-14049
[B]   CIP

First Edition: May 1999

1   3   5   7   9   10   8   6   4   2

To My Father, Joseph,
For the example of his life and who
throughout it all remained
scrupulous to his principles,
and
To My Wife, Rosalie,
Who married me for better or for worse,
and who for forty-three years
took both with confidence and strength